W9-BXN-329

TOOLS FOR CAREGIVERS

- **ATOS:** 0.7
- **GRL:** C
- **WORD COUNT:** 42

- **CURRICULUM CONNECTIONS:** animals, habitats

Skills to Teach

- **HIGH-FREQUENCY WORDS:** a, are, big, has, have, I, is, it, its, mom, see, they
- **CONTENT WORDS:** baby, calf, ears, eats, elephant, feet, follows, mouth, skin, sprays, toenails, trunk, wrinkles
- **PUNCTUATION:** exclamation points, periods
- **WORD STUDY:** long /a/, spelled ay (sprays); long /e/, spelled ea (ears, eats); long /e/, spelled ee (feet, see); long /o/, spelled ow (follows); compound word (toenails); multisyllable words (baby, elephant, follows, wrinkles)
- **TEXT TYPE:** information report

Before Reading Activities

- Read the title and give a simple statement of the main idea.
- Have students "walk" though the book and talk about what they see in the pictures.
- Introduce new vocabulary by having students predict the first letter and locate the word in the text.
- Discuss any unfamiliar concepts that are in the text.

After Reading Activities

Ask the readers to name the different parts of an elephant mentioned in the text. Have them draw and color an elephant calf. What color is it? Don't forget the long trunk, big ears, and toenails. How does an elephant use its trunk? Have each reader show his or her drawing and explain what the elephant is doing in the drawing.

Tadpole Books are published by Jump!, 5357 Penn Avenue South, Minneapolis, MN 55419, www.jumplibrary.com

Editor: Jenna Trnka **Designer:** Anna Peterson

Photo Credits: Michael Potter11/Shutterstock, cover; GroblerduPreez/iStock, 1; Alexey Osokin/Shutterstock, 2–3, 16tl; age fotostock/SuperStock, 4–5; Jurgen & Christine Sohns/Getty, 6–7, 16tm; Ralf Geithe/Shutterstock, 8–9, 16br; Independent birds/Shutterstock, 10–11, 16tr; GoDog Photo/Shutterstock, 12–13, 16bm; Exactostock-1598/SuperStock, 14–15, 16bl.

Library of Congress Cataloging-in-Publication Data
Names: Nilsen, Genevieve, author.
Title: Elephant calves / by Genevieve Nilsen.
Description: Tadpole edition. | Minneapolis, MN: Jump!, Inc., (2019) | Series: Safari babies | Includes index.
Identifiers: LCCN 2018024751 (print) | LCCN 2018027521 (ebook) | ISBN 9781641282369 (ebook) | ISBN 9781641282345 (hardcover : alk. paper) | ISBN 9781641282352 (paperback)
Subjects: LCSH: Elephants—Infancy—Juvenile literature.
Classification: LCC QL737.P98 (ebook) | LCC QL737.P98 N55 2019 (print) | DDC 599.6713/92—dc23
LC record available at https://lccn.loc.gov/2018024751

ELEPHANT CALVES

by Genevieve Nilsen

TABLE OF CONTENTS

tadpole
books

calf

I see a calf.

It is a baby elephant!

mom

It follows mom.

See its ears.

ears

They are big.

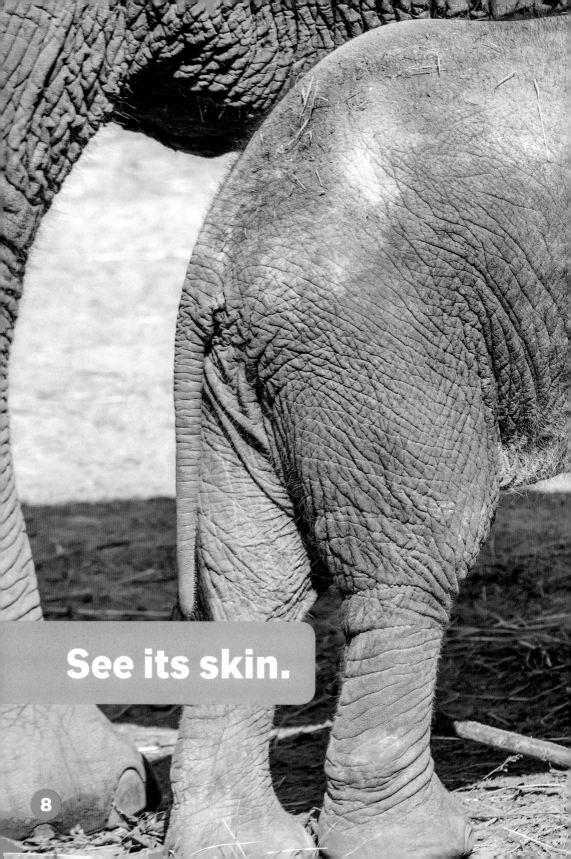

See its skin.

wrinkles

It has wrinkles.

See its feet.

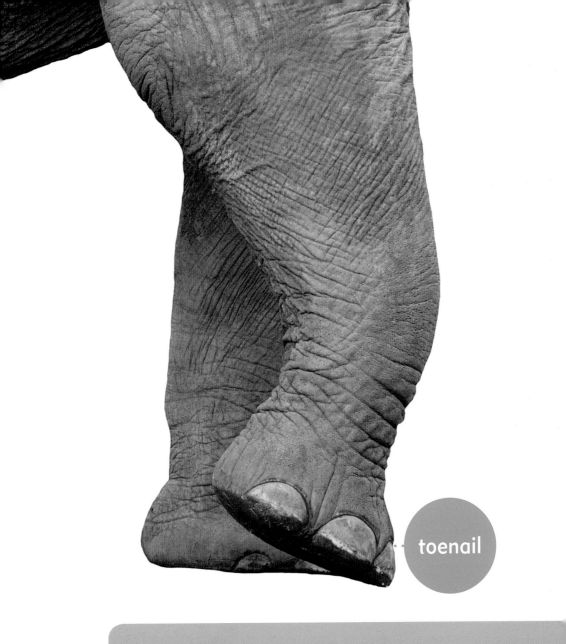

toenail

They have toenails.

See its trunk.

trunk

It sprays!

See its mouth.

It eats.

calf

ears

feet

mouth

trunk

wrinkles

INDEX